I0487022

ON HETERODOX AESTHETICS:

ANALOGICAL RELATIONS BETWEEN ARTS AND LOGICS

Maria Francisca Carneiro

Bloomington, IN 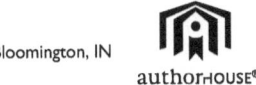 Milton Keynes, UK

authorHOUSE®

AuthorHouse™
1663 Liberty Drive, Suite 200
Bloomington, IN 47403
www.authorhouse.com
Phone: 1-800-839-8640

AuthorHouse™ UK Ltd.
500 Avebury Boulevard
Central Milton Keynes, MK9 2BE
www.authorhouse.co.uk
Phone: 08001974150

© 2007 Maria Francisca Carneiro. All rights reserved.

*No part of this book may be reproduced, stored in
a retrieval system, or transmitted by any means
without the written permission of the author.*

First published by AuthorHouse 3/6/2007

ISBN: 978-1-4259-9734-2 (sc)

Printed in the United States of America
Bloomington, Indiana

This book is printed on acid-free paper.

To my daughter Maria Fernanda Loureiro.
Acknowledgments to Dr. José Dantas Loureiro Neto.

Contents

1. ON THE POSSIBILITY OF HETERODOX AESTHETICS: AN ANALOGICAL ESSAY

ABSTRACT

This work deals with the analogical relationships between the philosophy of arts and heterodox logical foundations. Heterodox logic, a concept originally formulated from logic systems, implies in proper ways of thinking, perceiving and handling paradox or contradictions. From this idea in this essay we formulate some aspects of a heterodox aesthetics, focusing on the preliminary approach to the method, the object, the language and the basic concepts applied to this research.

1.1 Preliminaries on the method and use of language

This work proposes to make an analogical reflection in which some concepts of logic may help in quests of a philosophical character that are in this case, the main object of attention.

Obviously, this is not an easy task for, when trying to apply concepts of logic to aesthetics we discover the existence of a kind of ideal and linguistic gap separating scientific from humanistic culture. The clear arguments of science seem to become blurred when transposed to humanities, and expressions qualified as objective seem to loose all meaning. Because of that, we shall not transfer concepts directly from one branch of knowledge to the other since this would cause many distortions, ambiguities and an unsustainable series of indeterminations. We shall however, establish the relationships indirectly by means of analogies[1], in order to minimize the sometimes abrupt hiatus between these branches, as will be seen in the course of this communication.

On the other hand, an essay of this kind may in a sense be considered at a level of self-language (or specific language) somewhat more abstract and rarefied than the knowledge it is based upon.

In this sense, it is to be observed that the methodology of this essay in connection generically to relationships, transitivity, and connections between ideas and concepts, becomes altered with reference to the normal use of traditional methods of academic works specifically relating to the practice called by theories as grammatical or philological exegesis (notwithstanding the tautology of the words composing these expression's synonimy).

Let us adopt in this introductory part the definition of hermeneutics as the theory of the operations of comprehension in its relation with the interpretation of texts. Let us also adopt the distinction between comprehension and understanding, the latter being characterized by the logical-rational inferences of the cognizant subject in relation to the object; while in comprehension the subject includes itself in the object, with different results in the interpretation of the text. Still although in the act of comprehension there occurs a kind of fusion between the subject and the object, we must point out that this is not our way of thinking in regard to the production of knowledge.

Concerning this study about heterodox aesthetics, at the moment of formulation of knowledge or art, let us admit that the subject has a distinct and independent existence from the object, so as to preserve the concept of person and human personality and to distinguish him at first, from manufactured products. Obviously, the concept of person is constructed not only by a stagnant individuality, but considers interaction with the environment, society, and culture.

Even when, in a second moment, the object of aesthetic knowledge extrapolates the sphere of action of the subject by whom it was created and acquires an autonomous existence in society, we consider that this autonomous and independent existence of the object co-exists simultaneously with its relation with the subject by whom it was created in a previous moment.

By analogy, we may call this concept: *heterodox* in the sense of bearing, between a true and a false alternative, the possibility of both being true or both being false.

Besides the fact that in this question the much-celebrated problem of axiological neutrality is to be found implicitly, it is necessary to establish the present definitions as essential preliminaries to the reading of this essay.

I would like to begin this study by remembering an excerpt by Aristotle in the Prologue of his Ethics to Nicomaco when he says that we should not seek the same rigor in all discussions, and neither can we demand that from artistc productions. Therefore, we must limit ourselves when dealing with similar matters and starting from similar principles, to show truth in unrefined and approximate ways since it is a characteristic of the cultivate man not to expect rigor for each kind of thing but within the measure allowed by the nature of each matter.

Because of this, litteral exegesis does not appear to be the most adequate interpretation of this writing. Dissection of vocables and concepts aiming at objectivity, which are characteristic of science, would end up by occasioning some kind of reductionism, since total objectivity would certainly be illusory. The nature of the matter we are discussing bears significant parts of subjectivity which in a sense, may be inherent to the nature of matter.

However, the use of one or any other hermeneutics implies always the discipline of the spirit and in some cases, the rupture of some of the conditionings thanks to which knowledge has been refined and, certainly, has made progress.

This essay does not aim at uniformity on the use of language. Similar to mosaics or *vitraux* where refraction of light produces different prisms, or like in a supposed symphony where adagios, andantes and allegros and other movements compose in their own way and through their differences a final result, in the same way does this study utilize a language in which words should not be indistinctly analyzed as if by some chance and on a same level of equality, they bore some form of mathematical precision. They should indeed be understood in a contextual way, as much in terms of preceding warnings as in terms we shall examine in subsequent sections. For these reasons, this study is halfway to philosophy and litterature, therefore being more distant from science.

2.2   Basic concepts adopted in this essay: aesthetic, paradox, heterodox logic

Although the word **aesthetic** is usually used to designated the philosophic knowledge of art and beauty (and this is a restrictive acception of the concept), it is worth noting that other wider denominations are possible.

Some research in the field of the theory of knowledge about the capacity to make judgements, of organizing mental representations of tangible objects; and in the field of hermeneutics or theory of interpretation, research on the patterns of taste and cathartic connections as well as those of referentials called *poiesis* – that orient paradigmatic interpretations of each time and place, are also denominated **aesthetics.**

Moreover, there are concepts of that term of a more subjective nature such as those who understand the aesthetic element as the feeling to which thought adapts itself. In this sense, the field of aesthetics and the positive organizations of thought would be reflexive and reciprocally self-referent. There are still other meanings for the word **aesthetics.** That will not be considered here since they are of no value in this study.

As a unifying term of the variety of definitions attached to the word **aesthetics,** there is the ethymology of the word *áistesis*. To the greeks, *áistesis* was a special kind of feeling, a perception of reality which resulted in some emotion or sentiment. Thus, from "alpha privative" as negation, the word **anesthesia** results, understood as the abscence of that peculiar way of feeling. We can then affirm "grosso modo" that aesthetics motivate the study of the objects and aims described in the preceding paragraphs.

However, *áistesis* is not a unitarian or monolithic concept in the sense of apprehension of only one type of feeling, impression or emotion by the perceptual system of the human mind. That is why it is also possible to speak of an aesthetic of time.

Reflections on this subject go back to the concept of time. There are diverse concepts of what this dimension can be. It is possible to speak of "absolute time" as physicists do; of "linear time" measured by spaces and frequencies or intervals; of "intensity time" or "life time", that some of the primitive african tribes call "strong time" and "weak time", this oscillation occurring in proportion to the intensity of emotions.

Still, for the ancient greeks, the apprehension of time in *áistesis*, is not analytical in the sense that "aesthetic time" cannot be divided, decomposed in parts, constituting what is conventionally called "apprehension by totality".

In short, "apprehension by totality" may be understood as an immediate impact that overcomes us when seeing something beautiful. For example: when opening a window and suddenly seeing a sunset, we will be invaded by a perhaps extremely brief sensation – *áistesis* – which comes to us as a whole. At that moment there is no analysis or reasoning. It is only later when we are free from "*áistesis*" that we shall analyse the spectrum of the sunset colors, the physical phenomenons that make it happen, and so on. Good examples also are the vision of people we find beautiful and most of all, the impressions we collect from works of art.

This conception of *áistesis* contribute to sustain partly the position of certain currents of art criticism that proclaim the analytic impossibility of aesthetics (preceding kantism in this sense). By the same token the exegesis of texts on aesthetics should not be admitted.

In this study, the term aesthetics will be used in all the ways described in the preceding text, varying according to the contexts to which their prefer. For example: when dealing with mental organizations and representations and further on, with some products of literary, pictorial and musical art, it will be up to the reader to infer in each context which of the acceptions described in these preliminaries are more adequated.

The term **paradox**[2] in this essay should for now be understood according to its usual connotation and not necessarily as a technique of **contradiction** understanding in this way the argument containing at the same time a premise that affirms and another that negates the same object or circumstance. In the case of heterodox aesthetics these objects may be for example, expressions of art; and the circumstances would be so called human paradoxes which are some of the dramatic situations widely explored by literature[3].

So, the way paradox is understood in this study has classical bases and for this reason we shall not at present consider the problem of the absurd. Paradox and absurd shall be treated in future works.

Heterodox logic is among the terms we are analyzing in these previous considerations, the one requiring most caution in regard to its conceptualization and usage. Actually, it is a simplified adaptation official adaptation deriving from the nomenclature of the logical systems called **heterodox,** which deal with the operation of contradictory logics without incurring in the trivialization of the theories. Nowadays, the state of the art of heterodox logic is evidenced by the development of several subsystems and numberless applications.

Thus, the scientific character becomes evident through the systematization of heterodox logic, the perfect demonstration of its mathematical constructions, and by its wide spectrum of application.

Heterodox logic is a science and as such it is also based on philosophic concepts, some of them being more general and others more specific, that some scholars of logic call **theory of science** also presented on a high degree of theoretical systematization. In this way, several concepts are the subject of study of the theory of the science of heterodox logic such as truth, rationality, belief, causality, history of science, inferences, implication, deductions, etc... No doubt, these formulations are only possible because of a philosophical attitude that offers a favorable atmosphere that fosters them, and interacts with them though reciprocal feeding.

Yet, since it cannot be denied that there exists a "philosophical attitude" subjacent to heterodox logic, even as to the theoretic systematization according to the terms formerly described, to it this study refers and considers as its main strength the possibility of admitting rationally contradictions or paradoxes.

1.3 On the possibility of heterodox aesthetics: concept and object

Starting from the scrutiny of the concepts approached in the preceding item, let us now reflect upon what may come to be a heterodox aesthetics.

We may speak of a heterodox aesthetics within a restricted acception, understood as the possibility of having a reading or renewed hermeneutic interpretation on the existence of paradoxes in the diverse modalities of art – music, painting, literature, etc. – produced in the course of history.

It must be remembered however, that in general paradoxes or contradictions are objects of diverse artistic products and aesthetic schools and therefore, are not an exclusivity of heterodox aesthetics. The main characteristic of heterodox aesthetics resides certainly, in the possible analogy between those paradoxes and logical concepts.

In that sense, heterodox aesthetics should verify the treatment being offered and the behavior of paradoxes that happen to be interpreted in products of known art, through analogies with logical fundaments. Still, this is a minimum hermeneutic, as we shall see.

A *vice-versa* modality of what was described above, would be a kind of "induction" of heterodox aesthetics and would consist in producing objects of art purposefully paradoxal, and then interpret them. About how to do this, it can be said that artistic production is not ruled by scientific laws or postulates but surges spontaneously from heuristic intuition. Nevertheless, there are wider fields for investigating heterodox aesthetics like for example, acting like a metatheory of existing aesthetic schools, in the sense of observing the way eventual intrinsic contradictions to works of art are treated individually, and between different works or schools of artistic thought.

To heterodox aesthetics may also be assigned a reflection of gnoseologic character, oriented toward the structure and organization of some forms of reasoning, the construction of images and mental representations in relation to the existence and to the way paradoxes work, as will be seen in future papers.

Of course, these themes have been the object of several sciences transdiciplinarily, for many centuries and may also be the object of a heterodox aesthetics that could contribute to an unexplored reading of these questions.

As a matter of fact, the study of paradoxes has logic as a main epistemic region, and a reflection on the theme under the prism of aesthetics can mean a transversality for some, or a transgression for others. In any of these cases, there is an analogic approach in order to allow more freedom to reflections and *zethetic* research, which do not necessarily subordinate to conventional academic methodologies.

In Heraclitus, the possibility to deny and to affirm at the same time does not constitute a contradiction but a double necessity. To classical logic, a proposition that is at the same time true and false is a contradiction and therefore, an absurd or an impossibility. Hegel, in his dialetic underscored the strength of paradox, pointing out that from the confrontation between thesis e antithesis the issue is synthesis and that is the function of Philosophy. Several other scholars have approached the questions, in diverse ways.

As we said before, in the last decades logic has opened a new chapter of its history with the heterodox systems formulated by scholars which permit to operationalize mathematically the paradoxes without trivializing the theories.

Yet, from an aesthetic viewpoint – since knowledge is not only reason but also art, perception, interpretation – what have we done with paradoxes? How have we thought them?

In the search for coherence, traditionally recomended by science, we have perhaps forgotten how paradoxical, contradictory, or imaginary it is. In the attempt to "coherent pluralism" as Bachelard[4] writes, we have provided in the conceptual formulations and in the organization of knowledge, arbitrary separations between subject, object, time, space, taxonomies and genders, so as if not to annihilate, at least to hide the existence, primitive and originated in the real-imaginary-irrational, of the paradoxes, as will be explained in the course of a series of studies that are now begun.

But aesthetic responses include perhaps cognitive elements that in the specific case of coming across paradoxes, may be explored from different points of view as for example, heterodox aesthetics.

In this way, a heterodox aesthetics of the paradoxical condition is not summarized only by a formalized expression, but who knows may consist of a certain essential art, since thinking of beauty might imply some kind of beauty.

In the aesthetic filigree of paradoxical concepts, interpretative work does not develop thanks to a simple and monolithic deductive process, but on the contrary: the formulation of heterodox aesthetics may demand from our cognitive activity work in a possible consonance.

1.4 Some problems inherent to the formulation of an aesthetic knowledge

Even when referring to the formulation of mental representations and thought structures, aesthetics, if it is an aesthetics, is not confused neither with psychology, neither with technique nor with neurosciences. Aesthetics, as knowledge of forms of apprehension of sensitive reality, is not a science: it is a philosophy.

When, more restrictively, aesthetics refer to the study of art, besides the assertion mentioned in the preceding paragraph, another one, also of an epistemological character, would fit: up to what point is it valid to discourse on the work of art, trying to decode by means of words that which should be expressed per se? When and how is verbal or written language effectively capable of translating, narrating or interpreting an aesthetic circumstance? This query, if taken to its ultimate consequences would end in "wittgensteinian silence" and even this essay would be relegated to the realm of the ineffable.

Yet, there are other theoretical postures about this. We may consider that decodefying paradigmatic structures (in the case of apprehension of an element) is effected through a series of transformations that simplify hard to understand elements by means of the corresponding grammatical or semantic procedures, this being one of the central problems of psychology and linguistics.

The fact is that every work of art, in order to produce the necessary effect on the spirit, must be envisaged from a determined point of view and cannot be supposedly appreciated in an absolute way but in a real or imaginary situation, conforming to that demanded by the work of art.

By the simple fact that any language (including the scientific one) is always a mental representation of a given object, we find that there is a common origin, a root which is the symbolic language, inherent to all languages. This is the intuition that presides to the writing of the present text and that, to our way of thinking, legitimizes the use of analogy as a method of approach.

1.5 Whether heterodox aesthetic presupposes a form of logicality

The answer to this question depends on what is understood as logic. Scholars conceive different positions concerning relationships between reason and logic: for the dogmatic position, logical and rational are coincident in a sense. For other positions, this coincidence does not occur. Logic at present is much more than the doctrine of valid interferences. Now, this means that simply adopting a specific concept of what logic is cannot be satisfactory unless it is updated.

In Science there are no dogmas, eternal truths that must remain valid in all realms of knowledge. Everything can be modified, enlarged, and enhanced by permanent criticism. These concepts mean not only to question it, but even reformulate it, deny it, demonstrating that the presuppositions subjacent to it are excessivelly naïve and should be or have already been substituted by new ones.

According to this exposé, we can partially accept, for heterodox aesthetics, logisticization as well as criticism[5]. Logicization is partially accepted as a function of heterodox aesthetics because, starting from it, interpretations and inferences can be performed (that this essay denominates "readings") whose validity however, cannot be demonstrated because of the analogical-philosophical nature (and not logical-scientific) of the subject.

In the same way, criticism is partially accepted as a heterodox aesthetic function because its *telos* is the questioning, the reformulation, the enlargement, but not necessarily only the negation or refutation of different theoretical postures.

Thus, we see that heterodox aesthetics logicize partially and criticize partially objects and circumstances if we admit the non-absolute use of those terms.

1.6 First conclusions

These pages can be read as an analogical essay, half-way between the philosophy of art and the fundaments of logic. At the same time that we deal with the *querelle des anciens et des modernes*, we look for, in a subjective way, not an equivalence or a correspondence, but an analogy between the aesthetic perception of paradoxes and logic, that is, a *mímesis*, in which the spirit accepts analogies knowing that there exist similarities: non-*mímesis*.

After all, what interests us in this kind of reading besides art's creative power, is more specifically the vigor of paradoxes in works of art, capable of making unusual the everyday occurrence and awake in us some kinds of perception and knowledge not obtained through pure reason.

More important than knowing whether art imitates life of if life imitates art is to catch the meaning of this expressions, their vigor, and their creative presence among us.

In that sense, it is possible through art, even if for a moment, to have the impression of harmonizing the imperfection of the world and the unfinished within each one of us: *aesthetics*.

Still, to say simply that it is an analogical essay doesn't answer the question immediately, since the concept of analogy is one of the most tortuous existing in the history of ideas, and much has been written and theorized about it, in several avenues.

It is not our purpose in this paper to reopen discussions about the meaning of analogy. Nevertheless, we shall define it in this work as a procedure of invention (in the sense of creating a new situation), and of argumentation (since it is about inductive reasoning based on existing similarities between known situations and therefore previous to the new one), corresponding to a formulation of the type "it is similar to".

A common mistake is the confusion between analogy and similitude. Similitude is the external and immediate likeness between objects; while in analogy we understand that the likeness arises from the concatenation of a reasoning elaborated on objects, and therefore creative, mediate, and it does not serve a function previously determined. This is the concept of analogy that is being expressly used in this series of studies about heterodox aesthetics.

2. ON HETERODOX AESTHETICS: THE PERCEPTION OF DEGREES OF ABSTRACTION, HISTORICITY AND TIME IN THE WORK OF ART

ABSTRACT

If we consider that art and also the knowledge of the world are representations of perceived reality we incur the serious risk of generalization and triviality, besides reducing heterodox aesthetics to a merely narrative activity. In this chapter we propose the existence of different degrees in the heterodox interpretation of works of art and in the aesthetic perception of time.

2.1 Foreword

In the last chapter "On the possibility of a heterodox aesthetics" we discussed some preliminary questions such as: object, method, besides some approaches on language and hermeneutics concerning this subject.

In the continuation of these studies, it is proper to see that our intention is not to formulate a "scientific aesthetic theory" although we hold in great regard the work of Ernst Gombrich, who was responsible for what is one of the most expressive attempt in this century, to establish a theory of art on scientific bases.

It is worthy to remember however, that science and art as criative processes are driven by a common force, which make us feel more at ease to theorize analogically on each one of them.

But we wish to clarify that this analogical theory is not exhaustive and does not propose to examine all the assumptions implicit to itself. By the same token, it does not claim for itself the job of describing the world either relatively to strictly narrative purpose of the thematic aspects, or to the plastic character of objects disposition. What we really aim at are successive approaches around the same object of which provide displacements of concepts and multiplicity of levels of analysis.

For those reasons we shall examine in this paper the problem of narrative in aesthetics theory and its tendency to generalization and sometimes to triviality. We shall propose the question of gradation of aesthetic heterodoxity as a possible way of solving that question and, finally, we shall see how these questions relative to narrative, historicity and perception of time in art, may suffer variations, according to the underlying logic of the subject who thinks of them.

2.2 A question from the heterodox reading of the history of art: generalization or trivialization?

2.2.1 Problem of generalization

According to what we saw in preceding sections of this paper, heterodox aesthetics can be understood as a new way to interpret paradoxes pictured by the objects of art, throughout history. In this light, its is up to heterodox aesthetics to analyze them, decode them, observe the way they express and behave themselves, and how they are treated and solved, looking for analogical relationships with the concepts of coherence and consistency.

At this point, we are faced with another item: it is necessary to verify to what point heterodox aesthetics does not become confused with a new historiography of art.

What can be affirmed is that it is possible that from heterodox aesthetics a new historyographical school for the arts may derive; but not that it is a historiography in itself since, as we have seen, its proposition is not simply descriptive but involves specific objectives of philosophical character which do not include all objects of art, without distinction.

2.2.2 *Problem of trivialization*

In the opposite sense to what was discussed in the previous topic, it is possible to consider the fact that sometimes when we determine to analyze by means of heterodox aesthetics, the paradoxes possible to be absorbed in works of art, we can verify that this proposition does not have definite limits but that it can be extremely "elastic", really plastic, presenting an incredible extensional capacity which, if taken to its ultimate consequences, could be extended to art as a whole with serious risks of trivialization, as we shall observe next.

Let us see: when we observe Monet's Cathedral floating in a bluish haze over Paris, we can infer that in that concept the artist wanted to pull it off the ground, to abstract it, transubstantiate it, transmute it and so make it transcend because that was probably the way he saw it. Good examples would be the melted watches of Dali, surging from a modified concept of time, invoked by the artist. Let us remember still the successive japanese gardens of Monet like increasingly abstract degrees from a perception of imaginary-reality. Following that line of reasoning we shall inevitably conclude that all art, in all of history, is heterodoxical because any artistic object may in that sense present some type of contradiction since all art is always a representation of reality. Pushing a litlle further this chain of deductions, we shall conclude that representations in the form of language and knowledge about the world, are also paradoxical. Then, if that were so, we would end by concluding that all knowledge and the world in its phenomenological sense, would be heterodoxical and this would be a grotesque form of reductionism, generalization, and triviality. We must observe on this point, that the idea of a heterodox aesthetics must be led by the concept of truth formulated in the fundaments of Heterodox philosophy of logics and that therefore, it is restricted to specific realms with specific purposes.

Otherwise, if we accepted that even the most classical definitions of art, like the "eternal novelty" lead us to a paradox, we would certainly incur in the problem previously mentioned.

2.3 On degrees of heterodox in aesthetic appreciation

There is much discussion in science on the problem of consistency, and it seems that the more open the question becomes, the more it develops. The elements of coherence; what are justified beliefs; what is certitude; the derivations of scientific argumentation; the contradictions as imitation of reality; the identity of knowledge and the logical energy of the contradictory, lead us to conclude that consistency can a chimera because in a complex world there might be no assurance that the experiences were always consistent.

In this context, Paradox[6] stands out as an important chapter of the theory of inconsistencies and this, in its turn, situates itself in the superior sphere of the thematic of consistency in science, as in concentric circles. In this study, we focus on heterodoxical thinking as the nucleus of reflection on paradox and inconsistency.

So we ask: is it possible to consider that objects of art (and even others, of general knowledge) possess different gradations of inconsistency? Or, on the contrary, is or not the object simply contradictory?

On the other hand, when we decide to do some kind of reading or heterodoxical interpretation of works of art (this is a subjective factor) we can infer that the solutions of the paradoxes are creative, tending to an extrapolation of the field where contradiction was favored. Or, in the majority of cases, in artistic activity, the paradoxal condition is maintained due probably to its fetish value and aesthetic vigor.

Up to this point then, we can consider there are at first two degrees for heterodox aesthetics: one in the field of the contradictory condition, and another that extrapolates it.

Besides, if we expect in heterodox aesthetics analogies with the logic that inspires it, we shall see that the several hierarchized languages compatible with the idea of gradations. Finally, we could consider that, if heterodoxity were not passible of gradations and only admitted "totally heterodoxical" objects (T); or "radically non-heterodoxical" objects (F), without taking into account the interreign that mediates between those two poles, it would in a way, be negating one of its main fundaments.

2.4 Intuition and intensity: for a heterodox aesthetics of   superfluidity in the experience of time

What is time, a contour of the world? What makes the intensity or the duration of an instant, of a moment? Is there in time or in intensity a fundament of reality?

The intimist duration always contains a certain degree of tension, and it is in that intimist time that philosophy or "pure thought" happens in the sense of being kept away from experimentation or empiricism. It is in that degree of tension then, that the world becomes reality in the phenomenological field of the subject, that it contours it with the features of its possible reason: and here all the strength of time condenses in the intensity of thought.

Within the time of thought exist other times in which we move, transporting ourselves and transporting the fact that was past, so that part of it is a present or a future and then becomes the real time of the subject, at that moment, in a certain representative sense.

In the fluidity of thought there is the plasticity of durations: we make the fold of the instant, dilations, inversions and compactation of spaces of time. We do the same with some intellectual actions that we may expand, pulverize, dilute or gather, in the exact measure of our concentration or intensity.

Thus, in the phenomenological optic of the subject, time may be a matter of intensity and be subordinate to it.

We shall call intuition the minimum intensity of thought. We can speak of homology of intuitions and of a certain symmetry between grouped instants; and we are immediately and wholly transported into time/thought/linear, and not anymore in time/intuition/intensity.

It remains to be seen whether there are contradictions indistinctly in those possible subjective dimensions of perception; whether the contradictions continue in one or another dimension, and lastly, whether there are several logics for the subject who thinks within time.

On a future occasion we can speak of hetorodoxity of extension, somewhat like Baudelaire's dream, made of an incomplete universe whose greatness resides in intimistic depth, where the terms *vast, illimited* and *immense* are the equivalent of breathing. If, in another way, we admit that conscience exists only because of an object by itself (*pour lui-même*), we will conclude for the exclusion either of the infinite or of conscience.

2.5 To conclude

From this brief colloquy on the temporality and gradation on levels of paradox in the interpretation of the products of art, we can infer how relative these questions are, and that their variations occur according to the optics of the subject that interprets them. On the notion of limits, that is, on the point to which the heterodoxy of an object of art may be aesthetized.

We can conclude that this notion must be drawn from a code – corresponding by analogy, to certain logical systems – that may even become so abstract that it may not necessarily keep an immediate relationship with the object it represents. The object to be substituted by the image may not be concrete: it may be a feeling or a virtue. In that case it is given by a metaphor, and in such circumstances it will probably appear as the most adequate means for certain kinds of expression.

As a result of these question we come upon the following reflection: if artistic forms are representations or metaphors of a vision of the world, to what world do abstract forms refer to?

Whatever the answer, it is clear anyway that for heterodox aesthetics the mastery and manipulation of the so-called analogous codes to logical systems is indispensable since it is the best way to detect, tolerate, and transpose the elipses and lacunes in the paradoxical interpretation of objects of art.

3. ON HETERODOX BEAUTY: A VARIETY OF PERSPECTIVES AND MOVEMENTS

erodox: le beau, le non-exploré, le non-touché et le vif aujourd'hui.

ABSTRACT

This work deals with the nature and merits of judgements of value in heterodox aesthetics, discussing the concept of "heterodox beauty", that is flexible and varied. The possibility of the existence of a negative heterodox aesthetics is considered, because the discussion on paradoxes includes the problem of negation. There are comments on aspects of heterodox aesthetics in the absurd, in literature, in tragedy and in comedy.

Maria Francisca Carneiro

3.1 Heterodox beauty and the problem of value in art

Axiology, as philosophical subject is traditionally sub-divided in three different disciplines; one of them is aesthetics. Therefore, any aesthetic reflection must necessarily go through the problem of value, since from the whole derives the part.

However, these concepts are originally of scholastic nature. Indeed, it was in the Middle Ages, more specifically in the scholastic period that the hierarchic position of aesthetics in relation to axiology was established, and consequently in relation to the problem of value. Still, it is not necessary that this subordination be maintained. Particularly in the case of heterodox logic philosophy, hierarchic orders are flexible and movements among them do not mean logic-dedutive impossibilities; rather the opposite: one of the characteristics of heterodox reasoning is, for example, to stimulate knowledge of differentiated consistency without their being trivial or necessarily rigid.

Do all aesthetic theories have to appraise beauty and even define it? Not necessarily. There are aesthetic analyses of the sublime, of terror, of what is tragic, comic, and of several forms of artistic expression of human feelings. Thus, aesthetics is not restricted to reflections on beauty but also on the ugly, the non-beautiful and non-ugly, among others.

Besides, it is necessary to take care with definitions as perhaps one of the problems of the formulation of knowledge may be an excessive attachment to etymological origins, a kind of linear philological love that, when determining a genesis also conditions an end, so as to cause a measure of immobility in the concept object.

Nevertheless, if heterodox aesthetics involves itself in the interpretation of paradoxes in the work of art in its possible analogical relationships with the foundations of logic, drawing conclusions on the way they are perceived and on the aesthetic feelings and sentiments they cause, we think it is interesting, in the composition of "heterodox beauty", to have the recuperation of the aristotelian concept of *thaumázen*, understood as amazement at the paradox, from which all philosophy derives.

On the problem of value in art, specifically in the case of heterodox aesthetics, we should keep in mind the nature of aesthetic judgements. Some terms like "nice looking" and "horrible" do not constitute facts and therefore are not capable of consolidating themselves as statements. That being the case, there is no sense in linking the validity of judgements to heterodox aesthetics *i)* to its full objectivity, *ii*) to a supposed generalization or hegemony relative to the analogic interpretation of contradictions in products of art.

The reference of validity in judgements in heterodox aesthetics is a kind of relation, because it is bound to the relevance of analogies made between readings of paradoxes in art and the fundaments of logic. Now, as that condition of validity implies the problem of coherence, vagueness and consistency and, when referring to a specific realm without the necessary exclusion of others, it presupposes the admissibility of diverse logic systems, it may be concluded that for "heterodox aesthetics" and consequently, for "heterodox beauty" it is not possible to expect a unitary and monolithic concept.

Because of this, it is incorrect to speak of one heterodox aesthetic; one should speak of a variety of perspectives and movements in that form of analogic interpretation.

That is because the proposition of heterodox aesthetics does not conform in terms of pure rationality (understood as reason over reason); but aims at a type of knowledge linked to the communication of emotions (reason over emotion) and therefore must turn possible a wide spectrum of approaches, as wide as the human capacity for establishing analogical relations between logics and arts. Because of this wide spectrum of possible approaches, aesthetics is not an article for use, to be fitted into a mental scheme of categories, but must be composed of elements of content, as otherwise it would be a violation of meanings in art.

Meanwhile, to say that a spectrum of approach is wide and in a first moment non-enumerable does not mean it is infinite. If we affirmed that all art can relate to all logic in the same degree of vagueness, uncertainty and inconsistency, we would be leading ourselves not only to an insoluble paradox, but to an unsustainable monism as well.

3.2 Questions for a negative heterodox aesthetics

Amid the several aesthetics schools we cannot omit considering the so-called negative aesthetics, that has as one of its main characteristics the critical reflection of historically held values and beauty. It is based in a general way on the School of Frankfurt, and especially on T. Adorno and W. Benjamin's views and therefore it is oriented toward philosophic perspectives of sociologic nature, post-marxist. It is certain that under that prism, questions of production of art, as to sense and value, assume peculiar connotations, interesting in their properties.

However, we must not mistake negative aesthetics for other movements like *Kitsch* (cult of the ugly), or *Bauhaus* (from whence might derive aspects of the Constructivist school and, more recently, the so-called "Disconstructivist"). Also, we must not mistake negative aesthetics generally for all other post-modern factions or vanguard like for example, the works of *Bricolage*. There is no denying that there is some similitude in the expression of these manifestations of art and aesthetics schools that think about them, in the sense that all of them, under the influence of the revolution of habits, invert, transpose, and see the inversions and transpositions of values, and among them beauty, as historically conditioned.

Yet, when speaking of heterodox aesthetics does it make sense to speak of negative aesthetics? Yes, there is a negative heterodox aesthetics with its own specific formulation that therefore is not mistaken for other aesthetic movements, whether with an analogous nomenclature or not.

Negative heterodox aesthetics is based on the logical concept of negation, more specifically of heterodox negation[7] and attends the analogical relation already described, being adequate to the method and objects treated in previous studies on heterodox aesthetics.

Yet, we must observe that negative heterodox aesthetics does not depend on mathematical rules or logical laws; but like the other segments of heterodox aesthetics, it refers to the interpretation of paradoxes and is an integral part of it, because the concept of contradiction itself implies a reflection on negation. In this case, under the perspective of negation, the notions of truth, deductibility and aesthetic coherence are altered when confronted with the optics of an "affirmative" heterodox aesthetics, as we saw previously.

3.3 On heterodox aesthetics in the absurd, in literature, in tragedy, and in the comedy

Each one of the artistic expressions of human feelings, when analyzed by different aesthetics schools undergo a rich variation of perspectives; for example: the sublime in Kant's aesthetic line is observed with rigor, purism, and is decomposed in distinct parts, clearly and orderly set. Still, under the phenomenological focus, the same sensation of the sublime caused by art is totally impregnated by a subjectivity that does not prescind the belief in the essences and does not exclude from reality the emotivity of the subject. And so on, we could verify how the reflection on the feelings and aesthetized sensations are passible of variations, according to the focus attributed by the different currents of aesthetics thought.

In the case of heterodox aesthetics of the absurd, we must firstly consider that the notion of absurd depends on the logical system to which it belongs. From the classical point of view, the impossible is a physical impossibility, and the absurd is a form of logical impossibility, i.e., a contradiction. It is not necessary to say how much that posture is altered, not only under the prism of heterodox logics but also according to diverse contemporary scientific theories.

Still, it is good to keep in mind that before the admissibility, through logic and science of what is classically defined as "absurd", in art this was already a level of representation with strong significations. Examples: the existential questioning in Shakespeare's Hamlet; Paul Gauguin's letters, where expressions like "deaf symphony" and in his painting, the distance between nuances of color, set the basis of an aesthetic composition that can only be understood by the analogical use of unusual subjacent logics. In the same way, the intrinsically contradictory dialogues of Ulysses, by James Joyce; the extrinsically paradoxical communications between the actor and the audience, in the Bertold Brecht's theatre of the absurd; as well as the extrinsically and intrinsically absurd speeches of Alice by Lewis Carroll, illustrate the impregnability of that category for the purpose of the aesthetic theory that is now proposed.

In tragedy, as is generally known, the presence of paradox constitutes an essential element, characterizing a kind of link in the narrative since the play will improve according to the intensity of *poiésis*, *mímesis*, *diégesis* and *muthus*, in their contradictory cores, where Sophocles' Aeschylus is a well-wrought expression. In this sense, tragedy when revealing human impotence before the circumstances, is distinguished from the epic and the heroic, in wich the will play a dominant role in spite of contradictions. Evidently, these artistic manifestations allow some analogies with fundaments of logic, either by the way linguistic structures are organized, or by the way paradoxical situations are considered.

In literature, several poems stand out as typically heterodox products of art, where some of them stop and remain in the paradoxical situations while others transpose the paradoxes in heterodox mode.

There is a strong semantic measure in such poetic language not only because it approaches the problem of paradoxes under the prism of affectivity but because beyond that there is an impregnated philosophical knowledge emanated from the expressive basis of poetry. Of course, these factors add up and result in a much stronger and cohesive expression than is usually found either in poetry or academe; but almost never in unison, as in paradoxical poems.

Still about poems, we see the aesthetically paradoxical description of feeling (for example). The original feature that most immediately comes to mind in this narrative is the resuming of the classical ideal, where beauty and love coincide (like, for example, in the Agape by Plato); whereas this coincidence is placed and assumed as contradiction. In some poems the paradoxical condition is – more than maintained – accentuated; in others, it is heterodoxically thought, elaborated, transposed. Effectively, it is an aesthetic approach different from the usual.

On the heterodox aesthetics of comedy it can be said that since Classic Antiquity, humor has been all along human history an object of aesthetical discourse. Inclusively, there are primitive archaeological records of cathartic connections effected by humor that are also aesthetic manifestations, as was seen in the first chapter of this study on heterodox aesthetics.

Traditionally, psychology establishes three factors that cause laughter: authority, sex and absurd. Let us add exaggeration to that trilogy.

In this section we shall proceed to a brief specific examination, in what concerns the optics of heterodox, of the aesthetics of humor.

So, the first question is as follows: what is and where is the analogical relation between logic and humor for heterodox aesthetics? One of the probable possibilities of analogy – that is certainly not unique – consists of a form of disparity and resides in a certain "exaggeration" in the "non-monotonicity" of some language constructions. We explain: there are possibly, consistent and inconsistent aesthetics subjacent to monotonic languages. But there are limits, contours, modes and forms that delineate the possible logicity of those languages and influentiate in certain way, their expression of beauty. When the steps from one language to another are too steep, forced, operating transposition with very abrupt gaps, it may occur that some feeling may happen for humor.

It is evident, as has been widely emphasized in the foreword of this essay, that we shall never find the logical rigor of science in an aesthetic analysis. Therefore, we can never be precise about the extension or other quantitative characteristics of leaps or hiatus in the transpositions between levels of language. However, nothing is to stop us to conjecture about them from the qualitative point of view.

Another approach to the heterodox aesthetics of humor can be made by way of the theory of argumentation. Let us start by the use of apagogic argument.

Apagogy for the greeks, or more specifically in Sophistics, may be understood as a practice that "decontextualizes" arguments from a given domain, thus modifying its position in that same domain, with different results for some types of "similar-sillogistic" operations where inversions occur between major and minor premises. It must be clearly understood that logic cannot be confused with argumentation because of the problem of truth, however much there may be strong aspects of intersection between these fields of knowledge.

So considered, apagogy does not worry about truth or validity but about effects like persuasion, surprise and maybe, about aesthetics effects.

Take the example, caricatures. In them the author maximizes, exaggerates, some characteristics – and this is a mode of decontextualization – aiming at causing effects of humor.

Therefore, when considering the possibility of a heterodox aesthetic language of humor, we should not take into account only the "non-monotonic" transit, but also the intercontextualization of the arguments of the discourse.

3.4 Final notes

We have seen during this paper how variations, movements and different perspectives are possible in the realm of heterodox aesthetics, so as to delineate the plural character of theoretical conception.

The fact is that there are no hermeneutic rigid laws or canons for heterodox aesthetics; yet it is possible to formulate analogies that subsidize the matter, giving support to differentiated aesthetic interpretations and that is where its originality resides.

In addition, the term "heterodox aesthetics" is not being used for the constitution of a statement but to express feelings and incite reactions.

For these reasons there is always a "fósfor" in this topic as an inalienable note to any hermeneutics.

The interpretation of contradictions in works of art is not limited of course, to the pure rationalism of logical functions. The aesthetic perception insists on being treated as such in its sinuosities, arabescs and fringes, where the conversion of concepts are variations of the work: poetry may become sculpture, and music can become movement. Concepts may be raised, split and reverted to each other resulting in an aesthetic and heterodox reading that is not made beforehand, but may be composed.

To compose, in the widest aesthetic sense, means to project, organize and dispose diverse elements ruled by principles or laws of equilibrium, proportion, unity, multiplicity, harmony, and rythm. To compose aesthetically is to organize forms in space, aiming at transmitting or catching an emotion or feeling.

One of the possible results of heterodox aesthetics may be a kind of equilibrium understood as the state of distribution of movement or of a pause, where factors such as configuration, direction, vastness, limits or the conspicuous absence of those same limits are mutually determined in the analogical interpretation of paradoxes in such a way that the whole assumes the character of the necessity of its parts, and in which the elements show a tendency to change places of form, in order to relate better to the whole structure of the system to whom they refer and whose dimension is characterized by multiplicity.

Anyway, as the best conclusion, we must point out that in heterodox aesthetics the subject does not "draw out a thought" from an empty case, nor is it pre-determined; but he thinks it and invents it in a gesture of creation and freedom.

That is why in heterodox aesthetics the contradictions in art or its paradoxes are not mere expressions of something; they are something, like elementary and authentic figures of the theory it self.

Footnotes

[1] BOUVERESSE, Jacques. *Prodiges et vertiges de l'analogie*. Paris: Éditions Raison D'Agir, 1999.

[2] There are several types and classifications of paradoxes, that can easily verified, for example: paradox of learning of *Mênon*, paradox of *Bertrand*, paradox of dichotomy; paradox of *Zenon* or of the motion less arrow; paradox of *Grelling* about heterologicality; paradox of strict implication; paradox of ideal information ideal or of the theory of confirmation; paradox of the surprise test, paradox of *Russell* or of the classes; paradox of *Allais* or of the theory of decision, paradox of *Berry*, paradox of *Burali-Forti*, paradox of *Cantor*; paradox of *Curry*; paradox of *Goodman*; paradox of *Hempel*; paradox of *Zermelo-König;* paradox of *Richard*; paradox of *Saint Petersburg*; paradox of *Simpson*; paradox of *Skolem*; paradox of *Tertuliano*; socratic paradox; sorites paradox; self-reference or semantic paradox; paradox of material implication etc. These classifications, however, will not be discussed in the present study because their inclusion does not alter the central theme being considered, and they could merely serve as illustration.

[3] In Aristotle, when in tragedy *diégesis, poiésis, mimese* and *muthus* are found in clear and perfect outlines, paradox emerges explicitly and in this sense, it can be understood as a focus in which reside unusual nexus of causality. Therefore it is with much precision that the philosopher circumscribes in the tragic-paradoxal character, the *methabolé* or transformation or transmutation of fortune. The aesthetic function of paradox may also be that of provoking the *thaumázein*

– i.e. the "wonder" – which for the ancient greeks was the at origin of philosophical thought and from which starts the process of reflection. In Aristotle, **Poetica**, 49 b 26-27 and ss.

[4] BACHELARD, Gaston. *L'intuition de l'instant*. 2a ed., Paris: Librarie Générale Française, 1992.

[5] There are other points of view about this matter, like Morris COHEN and Ernest NAGEL's opinion: "Determinar qué es lo que hace de un objeto algo hermoso, sublime o poseedor de lo que há llamado forma estetica es el propósito del estudio o teoría del arte, del cual forma parte de la estética, si bien esta última estudia también la belleza natural que no constituye el objeto del arte. Al lógico solo le interesa senãlar que tal estudio abarca tanto condideraciones fácticas, determinadas en forma experimental, como consideraciones puramente lógicas de coherencia". In *: Introducción a la lógica y al método científico,* vol. 2, item XVIII. 3. La lógica delos juicios críticos sobre arte – la crítica exclusivamente estética, 4a ed., Buenos Aires: Amorrortu editores, 1976, p. 198.

[6] On the concept of Paradox, see the references at last chapter "On the possibility of heterodox aesthetics: an analogical essay".

[7] The specific question of interpretation on negative heterodox aesthetics will be the object of future studies. For now, we are interested only in commenting the possible variations of approach that characterize the plural optics of heterodox aesthetics, and serve to exemplify the central thesis of this *thesis*, without developing at present, the theoretical minutiae of the

problem. The same will be done in the next *item*, when we shall be dealing with the absurd, the tragic and the comic.

References

ARISTÓTELES. *Poética*. [s. l.]

BACHELARD, G. *A epistemologia*. Lisboa: Edição 70, 1993.

_____.*L'intuiton de l'nstant*. 2.ed., Paris: Libraile Génerale Française, 1992.

BARBARAS, R. *La perception – essai sur le sensible*. Paris: Hatier, 1994.

BARTHES, R. *Mitologias*. (trad. de Rita Buongermino e Pedro de Souza), 9.ed., Rio de Janeiro: Bertand Brasil, 1993.

BECHTEL, W. *Philosophy of mind – an overview for cognitive science*. New Jersey/London: Lawrence Erlbaum Associates, Publishers, 1998.

BECKER, L. A. *Ars boni et aequi: a arte do direito como monolítico obscurecimento*. Comunicação apresentada ao colóquio Luzes da Arte, Belo Horizonte, 19.08.97. *In* Escola de Frankfurt no direito. Curitiba: CAHS, 1999.

BENJAMIM, W. *Origine du drame baroque allemand*. Paris: Flammarion, 1985.

BERGMAN, M. *Methaphorical assertions*. *In* The Philosophical Review, v.91, 1982.

BOUVERESSE, Jacques. *Prodiges et vertiges de l'analogie*. Paris: Éditions Raison D'Agir, 1999.

BURKE, E. *Recherche philosophique sur l'origine de nos idées - du sublime et du beau*. 2.ed. Paris: VRIN, 1988.

BURWOOD, S.; GILBERT, P.; LENNON, K. *Philosophy of mind*. London: UCL Press, 1998.

CARNEIRO, M. F. *Sobre a presença de elementos estéticos na teoria jurídica civilista: direito como ciência e arte*. Buenos Aires: Hammurabi, 2001.

DIAMANTINO MARTINS, S. J. *Bergson – A intuição como método na metafísica*. Porto: Livraria Tavares Martins, 1946.

EAGLETON, T. *A ideologia da estética*. Rio de Janeiro: Zahar, 1993.

ECO, U. *As formas do conteúdo*. (os percursos do sentido). São Paulo: Perspectiva, 1997.

FRANK, H. G. *Cibernética e filosofia*. (trad. de Celeste Aída Galeão). Rio de Janeiro: Tempo Brasileiro, 1970.

GARDNER, H. *A nova ciência da mente – uma história da revolução cognitiva.* (trad. de Cláudia Malbergier Caon),. 2. ed., São Paulo: EDUSP, 1996.

GOMBRICH, E. H. *A história da arte.* (trad. de Álvaro Cabral). 16 ed. Rio de Janeiro: LTC, 1999.

GUATTARI, F. *Caosmose – um novo paradigma estético.* (trad. de Ana Lúcia de Oliveira *et al*), 2ª reimp., São Paulo: Ed. 34, 1998.

GUZMÁN, R. A. *La música y el derecho: una comparación.* In: Revista de Derecho Portorriqueño v. 32, nº 1-3, Ponce, 1992.

HUIZINGA, J. *Homo ludens.* Torino: [s.l.], 1946.

KANT, E. *Crítica da razão pura – estética transcendental.* [s.l.].

KNEALE, W.; KNEALE, M. *O desenvolvimento da Lógica.* 3. ed. Lisboa: Fundação Calouste Gulbenkian, 1991.

LABARRIÈRRE, P. J. *L'utopie logique.* Paris: Edition L'Harmattan, 1992.

LYOTARD, J. F. *Lições sobre a analítica do sublime.* (trad. de Constança Marcondes Cesar e Lucy R. Moreira Cesar), Campinas: Papirus, 1993.

MACEDO, S. de. *Uma estética jurídica.* In: Revista da Academia Brasileira de Letras Jurídicas, ano XII, nº 12, Rio de Janeiro: Renovar, 2º sem., 1997.

MAFFESOLI, M. *No fundo das aparências.* (trad. de Bertha Halpern Gurovitz), Petrópolis: Vozes, 1996.

MAGGIORE, G.. *Estetica del diritto. In* SCIALOJA, Antonio (Org.) Scritta Giuridica in Onore di Francesco Carnelluti. Padova: Cedam, 1950.

MATRAVERS, D. *The paradox of fiction: the report versus the perceptual model.* In: Emotion and the Arts, Oxford: Oxford University Press, 1997.

NICOLESCU, B. *O manifesto da transdisciplinaridade.* (trad. de Lucia Pereira de Souza). São Paulo: TRIOM, 1999.

NUNES, B. *Introdução à filosofia da arte.* 5. ed. São Paulo: Ática, 2000.

OATLEY, K.; GHOLAMAIN, M. *Emotions and identification –conncetions between readers and fiction.* In: Emotion and the Arts, Oxford – New York: Oxford University Press, 1997.

OST, F.; KERCHOVE, M. *Le droit ou les paradoxes du jeu.* Paris: Presses Universitaire de France, 1992.

OSTROWER, F. *A sensibilidade do intelecto – visões paralelas de espaço na arte e na ciência – a beleza essencial.* 2. ed., Rio de Janeiro: Campus, 1998.

PENROSE, R. *Shadows of the mind – a search for the missing science of consciousness.* Oxford: Oxford University Press, 1994.

PIETTRE, B. *Filosofia e ciência do tempo.* (trad. de Maria Antonia Pires de C. Figueiredo). Bauru: EDUSC, 1997.

PLATO. *Great dialogues.* New York: Penguin Books, 1984.

RICOEUR, P. *Interpretação e ideologias.* (trad. de Hilton Japiassu), 3. ed., Rio de Janeiro: Francisco Alves, 1988.

_____. *Tempo e narrativa.* Tomo I (trad. de Constança Marcondes Cesar), Campinas: Papirus, 1994.

ROTTLEUTHNER, H. *Les métaphores biologiques dans la pensée juridique.* In: Archives de Philosophie du Droit, t. 31, Le Systéme Juridique, Paris: Sirey, 1986.

SALAZAR, E. L. *Sentido comun, literatura y derecho.* In: Crítica Jurídica número 4, Puebla, maio de 1986.

SCHILLER, F. *A Educação estética do homem*. (trad. de Roberto Schwarz e Márcio Suzuki), 3. ed. São Paulo: Iluminuras, 1995.

SHLAIN, L. *Art & Physics – parallel vision in space, time and light*. (reprinted from *The Mathematical Magpie*), New York: Quill William Morrow, 1993.

TURING, A. M. *Computing machinery and intelligence*. (Section 1: The imitation game). London: Penguin/Harmondsworth/Middlesex, 1981.

www.ingramcontent.com/pod-product-compliance
Lightning Source LLC
Chambersburg PA
CBHW021901170526
45157CB00005B/1910